# A Blanquito
# In El Barrio

—

# Gil Fagiani

RAIN MOUNTAIN PRESS
NEW YORK CITY

Price: $10.00

ISBN: 0-9802211-3-7

Rain Mountain Press, 68 East Third Street, Suite 16, New York, New York 10003
www.rainmountainpress.com

**Layout and Design:**
David G. Barnett
Fat Cat Graphic Design
5139 Maxon Terr.
Sanford, FL 32771

PRINTED BY Publishers Graphics, Carol Stream, IL

ACKNOWLEDGMENTS:
Front cover collage: Jim Pignetti
Photographs used in art work: Richard Moreno

Library of Congress Cataloging-in-Publication Data
Fagiani, Gil.
A Blanquito in El Barrio by Gil Fagiani.
p. cm.
ISBN 0-9802211-3-7 (pbk.: alk. paper)
1. Drug addiction—Poetry. 2. Recovering drug addicts—Poetry. 3. Latin Americans—New York (State)—New York—Poetry. 4. East Harlem (New York, N.Y.)—Poetry. I. Title.
PS3606.A2655B63 2009
811'.6—dc22

First Printing: October, 2009

## ACKNOWLEDGEMENTS

Many of these poems first appeared in chapbook form in *Skidrow Penthouse* Issue Six, 2004.

Earlier versions of "Sweet Dreams in Spanish Harlem," and "Festival on East 102nd Street," were first published in *Off the Cuffs: Poetry By and About the Police,* (ed) Jackie Sheeler, Soft Skull Press, NY, 2003.

"Sticky Buns," *Skidrow Penthouse,* No. 4, 2001.

"Fluteflirting," *Medicinal Purposes: A Literary Review,* 2001.

"Blood Oath," *Mudfish,* No. 14, 2005.

"Maracas," "*Danzón Cubano,*" "Core," "Junkie Jig," "Ray Solos On the Title Cut from the LP Acid," *Skidrow Penthouse,* No. 7, 2006.

"Self-Portrait, 1968," *Medicinal Purposes: A Literary Review,* 2006.

"La Botánica," *Paterson Literary Review,* Issue 36, 2006.

"Hands-On," *The Ledge Magazine,* #31, Winter-Spring, 2009.

"Litany of San Vito," *Feile-Festa,* Spring, 2009.

"Water Games," *Writing Outside the Lines,* (ed) Tammy Nuzzo-Morgan, Peter V. Dugan, Wild Side Press, NY, 2010.

"Willie and the White Girl," "Muzzled," and "The Interview," *The Fox Chase Review,* Autumn/Winter 2009.

## OTHER BOOKS BY GIL FAGIANI

*Crossing 116th Street,* Skidrow Penthouse (2004)
*Rooks,* Rain Mountain Press (2007)
*Grandpa's Wine,* Poets Wear Prada (2008)
*Vino del nonno,* Italian translation of *Grandpa's Wine,* by Paul
D'Agostino, Poets Wear Prada (2010)
*Chianti in Connecticut,* Bordighera Press (2010)
*Serfs of Psychiatry,* Finishing Line Press (2010)

*I dedicate this book to Congressman Vito Marcantonio (1901-1953), and to the people of East Harlem—past, present and future.*

# A BLANQUITO IN EL BARRIO

**Beyond**

"*They are the ones.*
*The ones who drink silver whisky near the volcanoes*
*and swallow pieces of heart by the bear's frozen mountains.*"

"The King of Harlem,"
*Poet in New York,* Federico García Lorca,
translated from the Spanish by Greg Simon and Stephen F. White

"*Where is the voice of freedom,*
*freedom to laugh,*
*to move*
*without the heavy phantom of despair.*"

"Farewell From Welfare Island,"
Julia de Burgos, translated from the Spanish by Jack Agüeros

"*In the name of the mambo, the rumba, and the cha-cha-cha.*"

*The Mambo Kings Play Songs of Love,*
Oscar Hijuelos

# DANZÓN CUBANO

*To Orquesta Aragón*

Nineteenth Century melodies.

Violins stir the leaves of a mango tree.

Cigar smoke lingers in the air.

The tap tap of timbales, a blustery piano.

Surging string chorus.

Flute darts, dives, breathing white rum.

1966

# SHADES

He moved back to New York
from Minnesota
with his German-American wife.
Took back his name
from Archie to Arquímedes
researched his family roots
in El Barrio
grew a mustache
brushed up on his *español*
wore *guayaberas.*

Quit his job
at Chase Manhattan Bank.
Took a big pay cut
as director of a job training program
in a leaky storefront
on East 113th Street.
Hired José as his assistant
to help him out after his detox.

The barber's shears were missing.
José *no sabe na'*—didn't know anything.
The butcher's knives were missing.
José *no sabe na.'*
The electrician's and carpenter's tools
were missing.
José *no sabe na.'*
The typewriter, stenciling machine,
office furniture, copper telephone wire,
bathroom plumbing were missing.
*José no sabe na'*
and was goddamn tired of being asked.

The landlord shuttered the storefront.
José raged about losing his job.
Put the cops on to Arquímedes
because he wears sunglasses indoors.
Looks like a druggie.

# REUNION

Don Pedro makes enough money
as a butcher in New York
to relocate his wife Marisol and four children
from a wooden shack
in Caguas, Puerto Rico
to a railroad flat
on Park Avenue and 114th Street.

As a wife Marisol
never second guesses her husband
and as a mother
she's a stickler for tradition.
"*Bendición*—Blessing,"
her six year-old daughter Nilsa
says to her.
"*Dios te bendiga*—God bless you,"
her mother answers.
Call and response given
like at Mass
even if only minutes pass
since they last saw each other.

One morning
after Marisol visits an *espiritista*
Nilsa says
"*Bendición*,"
but rather than answer
"*Dios te bendiga*,"
Marisol grabs her hand
and takes her to Third Avenue and 110th Street
where they enter a building
and stand in front of a door

with a picture of Christ
and the words: *"Somos Católicos"*
pasted under the peephole.

Marisol knocks.
After a minute of silence
the door opens and Nilsa sees
her father in a sleeveless undershirt
sitting at a table covered with dishes.
Next to him is a woman
and two small children.
Her father gets up
but Marisol turns her back
and drags Nilsa away.

When they get home
Marisol screams
rips her clothes
rolls on the floor
until neighbors
call a cab
to bring her to the hospital.

Nilsa takes off her dress
slips into bed
and in spite of her friends' pleas
and her brother's punches,
refuses to move.

# Festival on 102ND Street

Mothers line up their kids
in front of a flatbed truck
with a merry-go-round
spewing black smoke
out of vertical exhaust pipes.
Women in hand-painted stalls sell
*arroz con pollo*, fritters, franks
*cerveza y bacalaito*.
Cops wearing seaweed-green sunglasses
lean against a wooden horse.
"What's this shit?" one says
pointing to a pile of *morsillas*
—black blood sausages.
A mob of teenagers
squeeze into a vacant lot
to hear a local band
shake up the humid air
with a chorus of four trombones.
Muchachos wiggle their fingers, hands, hips
to the boogaloo beat.
Somebody rubs against somebody else's *culo*
and a fight breaks out near the stage.
Cops wade into the crowd
swinging billy clubs
like machetes clearing a path
through jungle underbrush.
A man picks himself off the ground
throws a beer bottle
conking one of the blue-suited *macheteros*.
The injured cop holds his ear
calls in reinforcements
from the 24th Precinct.

The troops club another path through the crowd
trombones blowing louder
drowning out shrieks, curses
feet stumbling over brick rubble.

# CABRÓN

The streets are in the shadow
stage of dawn.
Manny, the no-count cousin
of the minister's son,
grabs my arm and tells me
a man carrying a big knife
just got called *cabrón*
and when an hombre
gets called *cabrón*—a cuckold,
*sangre limpia*—only blood
can set things right.

He pulls me down Lex to 103rd Street
ever the savvy ghetto-guide
titillating the college crowd.
In less than a year he'll be strung out,
locked in the brig at Fort Dix,
and hearing through the grapevine
that I'm bedding down with
his common-law wife Naomi.

I walk behind him
my nostrils rank with the smell
of cooking oil pouring out
of the Hollywood Restaurant.
The street light goes on
above Ortiz's Funeral parlor.
There are no murder mugs,
no *cabrón*-curses,
no big knife.

# CUCHIFRITOS

I had the sizzle in my chisel for Nilsa,
dug her big eyes, moist, meaty lips,
color and curves like sculpted teakwood.
One night I took her to Papo's *Cuchifritos.*
She'd been playing hard to get all summer long
and I figured a belly full of spicy pig parts and fritters
might open her up to other bodily pleasures.

I'd eaten *cuchifritos* once before
after a night of blowing weed
and tossing down Bacardi with Manny and Count
the former president and warlord of a local street gang
—"We even had our own social worker"—Count boasted.
We'd finished harmonizing such doo wop classics
as "Deserie," "Wind" and "Gloria,"
under the archway of the Park Avenue El
when Count pulled out a wad of bills
—birthday money, he claimed—and said,
"let's grit at Papo's," a *cuchifrito* joint on 116th Street.

Beneath blazing light bulbs over front window metal bins,
Count pointed to *orejas, rabitos, morcillas,*
*acapurias, pastelillos, rellenos de papa.*
Juggling white cardboard boxes dripping cooking oil,
we sat on car fenders and ate pig's ears, pig tails,
blood sausages, fritters and meat-filled potato balls.

The swagger of that night stayed with me
as Nilsa and I walked into Papo's
and copped squats on steel shiny stools.
I pointed to half a dozen bins
and soon *cuchifritos* were piled high in front of us.

Before I could pick up my fork
Nilsa grabbed a fire-red bottle
and bathed a *bacalaito*—codfish fritter—
with Louisiana hot sauce devouring it in three bites.
Then she picked up the tip of an *oreja*
and began to chew on the rubbery cartilage,
her teeth making loud crunching sounds.

Next she chowed down on two blood sausages
thick and black as a policeman's club.
Then she picked up a fried pig's tail
and ate it like an ice cream cone,
strips of pork sticking out the side of her mouth,
lips a blaze of yellow grease.
I sat quietly nibbling on a potato ball.
"What's the matter, *no tiene hambre*—
you're not hungry?"
I smiled as a drum roll by Tito Puente
blasted from the jukebox,
Nilsa keeping time by tapping
her knife against the side of her water glass.

# MARACAS

To Frank "Machito" Grillo

Rhythmic rain

of pebbles, seeds

against gourd skin.


Study in motion

of arms and wrists,

curves and thrusts.


Circles within circles

calculated to the *clave.*

The measure.

# LA CAPITANA

Seventy-three year-old
Iris Espinosa,
*La Capitana* for a local
antipoverty agency,
receives official notice.
Her petitions appealing
the cutoff of funds for children's
summer street program
have been denied.

Forget summer sprinklers
and closed-off streets.
Forget sixty-dollar stipends
for teenage counselors.
Forget spiced ham sandwiches
for children's lunches.
Forget trips to Central Park
and Randall's Island.

The day after a crowd of junkies
stomp to death a drug dealer
on East 104th Street,
steamed-up moms
and laid-off fathers
scream at kids:
"Keep away from *yerba* smoke
in hallways and courtyards!
Watch out for *tecatos*
in basements and rooftops!"

Along with ex-counselors,
*La Capitana* waits till
temperature hits 95 degrees.
Demands transportation money
from Gordo's Candy Store,

27

Bebo's Barber Shop,
packs Victor, Macho,
Little Johnny, Nyrma, Alicia,
Chucho and any other kid
she can get her hands on
into the Six train.

Getting off at City Hall
*La Capitana* buys
*todos los muchachos*
frankfurters with mustard,
onions, sauerkraut
and buys *todas las muchachas*
triple scoops of vanilla ice cream
capped with chocolate syrup,
nuts, and sprinkles.
*"¡Vámonos! ¡Adelante!"*
La Capitana hollers.
*"¡Hasta la victoria!"*
her troops reply.

On Chambers Street
the East Harlemites
charge into the elevators
of a gray granite building,
race past security guards,
scurrying secretaries,
mob executive office
maple and chrome shiny.
*La Capitana* bangs a desk
like she's playing the bongos
while white-suited men
pull on their ties
and stare at boys' franks dripping
on polished tables
girls' cones dripping on plush rugs.
"104th Street *presente!*
*Los niños* want their money!"

# First Day In El Barrio

It was our first day
in the neighborhood
a police officer with a smirk
and a hint of sideburns
escaping his cap
came to our door
and warned us to watch our step.
We were six students,
three men and three women,
wearing madras clothes, beards,
moustaches, shoulder-length hair,
on summer break
living in El Barrio
volunteers with
a local antipoverty agency.

Born in the Italian section
on Pleasant Avenue,
the policeman said
when he began his Barrio beat
he was young and idealistic too
and wanted to help people.
But in no time he learned
that except for a few residents
too scared to say a word
mostly he met backstabbers,
sneaks, junkies, welfare bums,
dope addicts and cutthroats.

We argued with him
brought up the twin evils
of racism and poverty.

He laughed, said we had too many
books on the brain
while he learned on the streets.
Before leaving he gave us his card
and winked at the women,
urging them to call him.

After the cop left
we sat around cursing him
for his cynicism
and hateful attitude
when we heard
the banging of steps
upstairs
and somebody shouting:
"¡*Me gusta!*
¡*Me gusta!*
¡*Me gusta!*"
"What does *me gusta* mean?"
"It means I like it."
We crowded on the landing
just as a young man
charged past us
with curly hair
olive skin
handsome as Sal Mineo
but with eyes popping out
and a belt dangling from his arm.
"¡*Me gusta!*
¡*Me gusta!*
¡*Me gusta!*"
he chanted
as he flew down the stairs
and out the building.

# 125<sup>TH</sup> STREET

I've been in El Barrio
less than a week
when I decide to take a stroll
to 125th Street
and explore
the northern border of the neighborhood.

Walking from the Park Avenue El
along 104th
I turn left on Lexington Avenue
past the *piragüero's* wooden cart
liquor bottles
filled with fruit syrup
a dirty rag draped
over a large block of ice.

At 106th Street a caravan
of cars drives past
covered with Puerto Rican flags,
horns blasting "La Cucaracha,"
girls in straw hats wave at me
with mocha tans
and strawberry fingertips.

I cross the street at 110th
and Lex
to avoid bare-chested muchachos
dragging people
cursing and kicking
from the sidewalk
into a gushing fire hydrant.

Between 117th and 118th
I see skeletal men
knotted handkerchiefs around their necks

walking in circles
heads down,
one holds a golf club
another an umbrella handle.

Radios blast
the maniacal mumbling
of Eddie Palmieri's *"Azúcar,"*
Ricardo Ray's brassy
"Jala Jala Boogaloo,"
the plunking
of country guitars.

I turn left on 125th
and reach a hot dog stall
under the commuter tracks
of the New Haven Railroad,
consider buying a frank
my stomach revolting
at the odors of grease,
garbage, and bus fumes.

Across the street
a white man gets out of a cab
wearing a yellow suit
with an ebony ascot.
When the door opens
to the Uptown Bar and Grill
he's greeted by women's laughter
and a steamy sax solo.

I'm one mellow fellow
high on molten expectations
when somebody rams into me.
I see a rally of men
in jackets and ties, hear
the crackle of a loud speaker.
"Wake up, clean up, stand up,
the white devil's day is over!"

# Fun City '66

Under the mist
of open
hydrants

a row
of car-sitters
watch

a woman
swat
a man

with
a vacuum cleaner
hose.

Shoppers
from La Marketa
stop, plead

but the woman
makes
like a whirlybird

silver hose
flashing
smashing

*aguacates*
*chuletas*
*huevos*

a hundred
laughs lifting
off fender seats.

# The Bon Vivant

Tall Chucky Ramirez
with crow-black hair
on taut copper face
*bien indio*—real Indian—
the locals say
trains Cornell student volunteers
at their first staff meeting
of the Barrio Tenants Council.

"You ain't here
to push your middle class values
on the people of El Barrio,"
he says, clenching his fists
shiny with gold rings,
"nor to teach the poor manners
or morality."

"You ain't here to raise
your grades in Spanish class
or to learn how to cook
*arroz y habichueles.*
You are here to listen
to the people of El Barrio,
to respect the people of El Barrio,
and to serve as a resource
to the people of El Barrio,
so they can grow stronger
and wean themselves
off the white power structure."

When the meeting ends
Chucky, part owner of the Bon Vivant
Night Club on West 57th Street,
lets the Puerto Rican secretaries
leave the room before inviting
the college gals to drop by his place
for a drink or two.

# ON MY BLOCK

a woman
sits by her front stoop
in a wheelchair
sunning
the festering stump
of her amputated foot.

On my block
a husband
with four kids
keeps his apartment lock
in his pocket
because he doesn't
trust his wife
out of the house
while he's humping
clothing racks
in the Garment District.

On my block
an alumnus
of the University of Havana
hides
*sobrecitos de manteca*
—little envelopes of dope—
in his hatband
while two doors down
his daughter
is on all fours
with the landlord's agent.

1967

# MY LATIN ROOTS

I'm in Venezuela

centuries ago

*elegantissimo* in a red

cavalryman's blouse

saber in hand

looking out a casement window

black smoke and flames

crackling behind me

the sun's gleam on the sea

like the blade of a guillotine

three hundred feet below

# Ray Solos On The Title Cut From His LP "Acid"

To Ray Barretto

Conga fury

smothers:

weaving bass vibe,

*clave* chops,

shrieking brass birds,

guiro rattlesnake.


Eyes closed

cut finger

*¡allí na' más!*

—*there's no more!*—

after tones painted in blood.

# SWEET STREAMS IN SPANISH HARLEM

The snow cone
seller's wooden cart
lies on its side

along Third Avenue
its shiny
turquoise paint

showing
the footprint
of the cop

who kicked it over
for unregulated
business practice.

Out of the mouths
of broken bottles
syrupy streams
of purple, green
and orange
inch their way

across the sidewalk
towards the Coloso
Furniture Store

where beds
collapse
upon human contact.

# Amigos

They sit in the Eagle Theater,
the floor sticky with chewing gum,
popcorn, *cuchifrito* wrappers,
air reeking of Gypsy Rose,
reefer smoke and cigarettes.
"Zombies in Paradise," is playing;
it's the first of a triple feature.

Augustín is half-asleep,
his head aching from swilling
all night with old friends.
He's only here because he told
his sister Nilsa
months ago he'd bring her to the movies
and he's tired of her nagging him
to keep his promise.

He wanted to go to Times Square
but it was a rainy Saturday
and he was lucky to drag his ass
the ten blocks to Third Avenue and 103rd.
His mother would be pissed
if she learned they went to The Eagle,
a place she called *un cagadero*—shit house,
but Nilsa won't say *nada*,
not if she wants to see a flick again.

The projector hums
like an electric shaver
and celluloid faces look rubbery
from rips in the screen.
All around winos and *tecatos*

slump in their seats.
From time to time somebody pushes
through an aisle
setting off a loud clacking from
bottles banging on the floor.

Augustín is about to conk out
when Nilsa screams
at a zombie munching the guts
of a surfer on Waikiki Beach,
the bloody intestines
hanging from his mouth
like buccatini
dripping tomato sauce.

A *tecato* behind them
skinny with a ratty white face
falls forward,
a lump of vomit
lands near Nilsa's shoe.
"Sorry amigo," he says,
wiping his mouth with the back of his hand.
"You're no friend of mine," Augustín says,
pumping two rights
into the side of his head.

The *tecato* rubs his ear,
shuffles out of the aisle.
Augustín sits back
yawns
closes his eyes
while Nilsa trances-out on
hungry zombies shaking humans
out of palm trees.

# Diddy Bop

The dip in the hip tells the girls
he could break into the slop,
the dog, the boomerang on a dime.

The dip in the hip tells the bros
he has mucho heart, mess with him
better reach for your shank.

The dip in the hip tells the teach
a lot under the cap don't mean
you walk with a stick up your ass.

The dip in the hip tells the heads
he could be carrying, but if you
wanna cop, get your money right.

# UNDER THE FERRIS WHEEL

I looked up to them:
Count—his real name,
Heriberto Colón Hernández—
warlord during the glory days
of aristocratic, street fighting gangs,
and Nandy—Dandy Nandy—
former second tenor
of the 103rd Street Latineers,
a guest once on Symphony Sid's radio program.

Together they'd schooled me
—college dropout, utopian do-gooder—
in the ways of the streets:
*la buena gente, la mala gente,*
the trustworthy, the honorable,
the whores, hustlers,
*títeres,* and cutthroats.

They taught me
how to slap five,
make verbal jive
*en español:*
*¿Qué pasa?*
*¡Vaya¡*
*¡Qué chévere!*
 *Estoy en algo.*

The best place to cop
*piraguas,*
*pastelillos,*
*rellenos de papas,*
*pernil* sandwiches,
bags of chiba-chiba,

cut-rate jugs of fruit-flavored wine,
Orange-Rock, Lemon-Rock,
Tito Puente and Machito albums.

Things to say to muchachas:
*preciosa,*
*tú me vuelves loco,*
*¡ay mama!*
But Count and Nandy changed:
long sleeves in 100 degree weather,
legs that couldn't stay straight.
They laughed less,
took off without warning.

I saw them together for the last time
at the Feast of Our Lady of Mount Carmel
on 3rd Avenue and 116th.
Squeezing through a crowd
of fine Italian and Puerto Rican mamis,
with a *cerveza fria* in one hand
and a sausage hero in the other,
I scoped them out under the ferris wheel
picking through weeds,
metal piling,
cardboard boxes of pizza crusts.

*"¿Qué pasa?"* I said,
a boss lid cocked over my left eye.
"Something fell out
when we rode the ferris wheel,"
Count said, white-lipped,
the bones of his shoulders showing.
"Like what?"
Nandy turned,
dropped to his knees,
staring through the holes
of a sewer grating.

# DIABLO

The fortune teller's parrot
picks out a card for me:
When one door closes,
another opens.
So after Nilsa shoots me down
I decide to put a bead
on her best friend Soraida.
I waste no time making a play:
bringing her to Don Quijote's
Bar and Grill for *arroz con pollo,*
checking out "Return of the Creature"
in 3D in Times Square,
taking her to Orchard Beach
where her cinnamon body
in a bathing suit
puts a torch to my testes.
But while I'm steaming
Soraida never catches fire.

Knowing she digs music
I take her to a street festival
on Park and 118th
to hear the Barrio All-Stars.
A circle has formed around
a skinny German guy with pimples
and a mop of red hair
who boogies with two muchachas.
Women clap and shout,
"*¡Vaya, Diablo!*
*¡Así se baila!*
*¡Sacude!*"

His name is Helmut Koenig,
but the devilish way he dances

has earned him the nickname *Diablo*.
As soon as I see the way Soraida
looks at *Diablo's* weaving head,
his shimmying shoulders,
his hips smooth as water,
I know I'm a goner.

My uptightness in public
keeps me in the shadow land
of back rooms
as soon as music plays.

After *Diablo* dances with Soraida
she declares herself *enchulada*
loco in the coco
gooey and goofy for *Diablo*.

Now I see them at parties,
*Diablo* with his liquid moves,
Soraida with limbs swaying
like leaves of a palm tree,
the cries of dancers:
"*¡Salsa 'na ma'!*
*¡Chévere!*
*¡Qué rico!*"
Then Soraida becomes pregnant
and her German-born *salsero* vamooses.

After Nilsa and I get back together,
then break up again,
I'm visiting a nurse friend
at work in an abortion clinic
and there is *Diablo*, skinny, pimply,
big mop of red hair
sitting next to a muchacha
in the waiting room,
his head moving to a syrupy cha-cha
flowing out of the radio.

48

# JEFFERSON POOL

We give ourselves a good
pre-swim tune-up in the park:
bottle caps of Don Q
sprinkled with lime,
frosty slugs of blackberry brandy,
*bombas* of African Black
spliced with hash,
sniffs of horse
and pimp's dust.
Our skin glows like the last
pink patches of dawn.

We reach Jefferson Pool
and strip down to our undies.
It's three hours after the official closing.
I climb to the top of the tall iron fence
and watch the tenements
fade into darkness.
Pat and Chino drop down
and dive into the water.

I remain at the top of the fence
surveying empty stretches of tile,
the blue and white water motion,
echoes of curses and threats
hurled at Puerto Ricans
when the Italians claimed
the pool area as their turf.

I climb down,
plunge feet first
into the tepid water,

my arms, chest, and legs tingling
waves of sugary vibrations.
Pat and Chino begin to cuff
the water at each other,
their teeth gleaming
in the moonlight.

I tilt my head
and see the blinking lights
of fireflies,
wishing they were
women's copper bodies,
mango and melon curves,
the saxophone of King Nando's "Fortuna"
wailing in the distance.

# THE JUNKIE JIG

"*Mama Güela*," Tito belts out
and Papo's legs twitch like bass strings,
his feet nailed to the sidewalk.

The brass climbs up the scale,
Papo snaps his head back,
eyelids flickering like trilled trumpet keys.

Timbales and congas go to war,
Papo's eyes close, chin on his chest,
hips humping three beats behind.

"*Mama Güela*," Tito belts out again,
and Papo's body, like wet cement,
lurches downward, quivering to stray static.

# CRAZY FOR CAL

To Cal Tjader

I beat the landlord a month's rent
to cop a front row ticket
at Madison Square Garden.

Called in sick at work,
I played from early morning
Cal's juiciest jams:
"Soul Burst," "Picadillo,"
"Afro-Blue," "Maramoor Mambo."

Notching my head up
for the vibratory ride,
I noshed on mushrooms,
smoked wacky weed,
sniffed paradise white,
sipped Baccardi Añejo.

The day after the show
I woke up to the skipping
of my phonograph needle,
head heavy as a truck tire,
two yellow concert tickets
peeking up at me
between the crack of my sofa pillows.

# LA LOCA

Hortensia raises three boys
on a block in East Harlem
with more rubble piles
than standing buildings.
She works as a secretary
at the Barrio Tenants Council,
never missing a day,
never a minute late,
her long slender frame
always neatly hidden
in a charcoal business suit.

At home she kicks out
her dope-deranged husband
and changes the locks
to keep him from pawning
the refrigerator or stove.
One night her youngest son
shits on himself
when he finds a masked man
trying to pry his window open
and recognizes his father.

Still the kids excel at school
and Hortensia is saving money
to move off the block.
Many men at her job have asked her out
but she turns them down,
saying she prefers to wait
until the kids are older,
her discipline and decorum
the stuff of local legend.

When Saturday comes
Hortensia bundles off her children
to her mother's in the Bronx
and changes into a flimsy
flamingo chiffon gown
spotlighting her chocolatey tan,
*mucho* shoulders,
*mucho* cleavage,
*mucho* thighs.

Then in her friend Belén's car
she burns her first bone of the night:
*sin semilla*—seedless Colombian buds.
Hortensia' s eyes blaze,
her body rocks.
By the time she steps into the Hunts Point Plaza
and hears the timbales and trumpets
her *hombros* and *cintura* are churning.

The leg-men and pretty-boy dancers
are all waiting—not for Hortensia—
who's Hortensia they ask?
But *La Loca*
the slender whirlwind
who dips and dives to the bass vibe,
—"*¡Así camina La Loca!*" someone shouts—
hair flying, lips trembling,
brown limbs blurring
to the conga's blistery beat,
—"*¡Así camina La Loca!*"

# MANTECA

Shoveling heaps of greasy white powder
up my sneeze box with Lefty
under an umbrella in the park on 108th Street,
the rain falling, our knees buckling,
Dizzy Gillepsie shouting in my head
*Man-teca!*

Loamy smell of wet sidewalks
seeps into my lungs,
soft waves of warm summer shower
carry me to Park Avenue and 114th.
The El gleaming like onyx,
trombones and saxophones celebrating
the first time I've taken a taste
of *man-teca.*

Swaying to the tinny drumbeat
under the overhang of Manny's Bodega,
I look up at Nilsa's empty window,
our laughter, sitting butt cheek
to butt cheek on rusty car fenders,
hasty kisses in pissy hallways,
the time her mother slapped her
for disappearing in the park with me,
my stomach sinking,
*man-teca.*

1968

# My African Roots

Chaos in Katanga.
I poison wells, smuggle guns,
dump dead jackals in front
of rival chieftains' houses,
snuggling up to a grass skirt
when vultures cover the ground.
Then a strongman emerges.
The people want order.
In a fight, I trample food piles,
smashing clay pots, the strongman
throws his ax, killing my opponent.
I flee by ship to Tierra del Fuego,
work my way through Latin America
until I'm on a subway in Harlem,
kids playing the dozens.
A cop's been killed, one of them says.
I get off in front of a porn theater,
"The Ebony Enchantress."

# WILLIE AND THE WHITE GIRL

Laid off after 24 years at Bub's Lumber Yard
Eliezer Loggins moves
from Biloxi, Mississippi to the Big Apple
with his two sons and ends up
working as a super on a three-floor
walkup on East 108th Street.

Nine months later he sits on his front stoop
wearing his straw hat,
a can of Pabst Blue Ribbon in his hand,
doing his best to understand
what is going on around him.
It all seems cockamamie:
the constant fires and break-ins,
the surging traffic and sidewalks,
the radios blasting in *español,*
the kids who stay out all hours of the night.

More than anything he can't
figure out what happened to his two boys:
Bobby—now known as Bosco—
drinks wine all day
and has already been locked up twice
for stealing and fighting.
Willie, the boy who a Southern minister
said had a heart of gold,
spends all day chasing after some white powder.
Where had he and his wife gone wrong?

Two months ago, Mr Loggins put a whumping on Willie
and threw him out in the street
after he caught him picking through his wallet.

But he couldn't stand seeing him sleep
in the alleyway
and let him stay in the basement
on a bunk made of wooden boards
on the earth floor by the furnace.

What really stumps Mr. Loggins
is the white girl who stays with Willie,
not a day more than twenty,
light yellow hair like margarine on spaghetti,
blue eyes in muddy pouches,
plump in spite of the black staples
running up and down her arms.

Willie calls her Pinky
and it's Pinky that now brings him
his white powder.
Whatever she's doing to get it
is grinding her to dog shit.
Willie just stays in the cellar,
his body frozen at the corner of his bunk,
his shaved head like an oily eight ball,
his lower lip hanging down.
That's how Mr. Loggins finds him
when Pinky comes to tell him
that Willie won't wake up.

# The Bathroom at the Village Gate

Johnny Pacheco *y Su Tumbao*
rouses the dancers
but not as much
as the bathroom door.
When it opens *bailadores*
break their stride,
ditch their partners.

The signs that read:
"Madame" and "Monsieur"
mean nothing, unisex
and multiple admissions
are the norm: two men,
three women, men and women
all in the same room.

And fists pound
the locked doors
if the occupants dawdle.
From inside swirls of smoke,
perfume, and zoo sounds:
bird whistles, hog snorts,
hyena laughs.

Then the doors open,
the tide reverses,
dancers with rosy eyes,
runny noses,
rush towards
the rollicking horns
and Johnny's maracas.

# POINT BLANK

The heads have been hungry
and after dealing in the park all day
Pat has a wad the size of a sandwich.
We take one last swig, smoke, snort,
jump into a Checker cab
and make it down to Times Square
to see "Point Blank" for the 10th or 11th time.

The Victoria Theater is near-empty
and smells like a dog pound in August.
We wrap our feet over the seat
in front of us, pass back
and forth a brass pipe
stuffed with hash and reefer
and cackle and guffaw through
a half dozen coming attractions.

Then a scan shot of Alcatraz,
gun shots, a cell door slams shut,
deafening heel clacks.
Some tourist-type behind us
complains he can't see through
the hedge-high cloud of reefer.
Pat holds up his middle finger
"If you don't like it, mothafucka, leave!"

An apartment door bursts open,
four bullets scorch an empty mattress,
rants about revenge
and recovering $90,000.
Pat cracks a sack of tragic magic
and with bent matchbooks
we feed our flaring nose holes.

Time drags on through a haze.
We nod to the backdrop
of a soul singer's wails in a night club,
his mouth stretching across the screen.
Punches to the balls,
beaten body tossed
into a metal food rack,
blood dripping like catsup.
"Holy crap," the tourist mutters.
I get up to drain the lizard,
walk a long corridor
where a black giant has his foot on the wall
blocking my way into the crapper.
After a minute or two the giant
lowers his leg but I decide
to go back to my seat.

When I return a man sails
out a hotel window,
a head gets whacked with a pool stick.
Bridges, highways, cement waste land,
pipe-smoking sniper kills, and kills again.
Final scan of Alcatraz.
Pat passes me a corner of coke.
I sniff directly out of the glassine bag,
the tourist behind glaring at us
as I wipe my nose with my hand.

# LEFTY

Lefty's skin glowed golden brown
when he first came out of the joint.
He'd been my roomie Pat's cellmate
and I liked the way he wore
his oyster-colored cap cocked to the side,
his warm baritone laughter,
the way he'd say, "That's deep," whenever
he agreed with something I said.

He'd grown up in El Barrio
and had no fear of the streets.
Once in Times Square
two punks tried to rob me at knife point
and Lefty came over with his hand
in his jacket pocket
saying he was packing a heater
and sent the punks running.

Lefty gave me my wings
—my first shot of *caballo*—
on a rainy day
under an umbrella
in the park on 108th and 3rd,
the same park where I saw him stab a guy
twice with a bread knife
for selling him beat dope.

After he got hooked on horse
he took me to his folks' house
to hustle some money.
His father had been bingeing
for two weeks on Seagram
and when he learned I was Italian
he started swinging at me
screaming "¡*Perros italianos!*"
until Lefty jumped between us.

Then Lefty's horse habit
trampled his brain,
made him break into our crib
robbing my knit shirts
and Pat's alligator kicks.
When I saw him months later
during the riots
that ripped up Third Avenue
his arms were bandaged to his elbows
from poking through
broken store windows.

Then he began to stick up drug dealers—
he knew all their spots
and he'd show up with his bread knife
and demand *material*—drugs
and *plata*—money.
He'd hit solo dealers
and syndicate dealers
and soon his victims got together
and put out a contract on him.

The last time I saw him was in a bakery,
skin like rancid butter
all bug-eyed
asking me if I'd seen the *cañoneros*
looking to give him the rub.

Two weeks later he was marched
to a rooftop
and plugged so many times
in his face that they kept
the casket closed at his funeral.
Somewhere inside
I heard hoofs
pounding to kick the lid open.

# DOPE SCOOPERS IN EAST HARLEM

For the poor:                folded matchbook cover

For the athletic:            gym locker key

For the literate:            BIC pen top

For the dandy:               chrome nail file

For the nouveau riche:       necklace-held gold spoon

For the femme-fatal:         long polished fingernail

For the vicious:             linoleum knife blade

# SHAFT SHOT

In 1966 I spent the summer
chasing after Nilsa
because her mother told her
to stay away from me,
that the *blanquitos* only want one thing
and when the summer's over
they're out of the hood.

After I gave up on Nilsa
I rented a railroad flat
in El Barrio,
hung out with the park crowd
on 108th and Second
and in short order went from
chilled pints of Gallo Port,
to pot, pills, rum, hash, coke
ending up with a snorting jones on *caballo.*

In the spring of '68
Nilsa phoned me
and a week later
skipping the prelims
we hit the sack.
She told me it was her first time
and I believed her,
my bed sheet stained green
and the smell of mint in the air.

She said she trusted me
and that she'd always
been terrified of sex
because when she was ten
she saw a *tecato*
with scabs covering his arms
drop his drawers in her courtyard
and take out his thing
big and bent as a turkey neck
and after cooking up his dope
in a blackened wine cap
shoot up in his shaft.

When he finished
he pulled his pants up,
closed his eyes,
threw his head back,
jumped around for a while
then disappeared through a doorway
while she gagged
climbing the stairs.

Nilsa was trembling
when I rubbed her back
kissed her forehead
and went into the bathroom
running the faucets
to hide the sound of my taking
a snort or two
to hold down my habit.

# SELF-PORTRAIT, 1968

Black hair curls
out of green Kangol
with cigarette-burned brim.

Jaundiced skin
hosts daddy longlegs
goatee and moustache.

Wine-stained shirt
jammed fly zipper
hollowed-out heels.

In back pocket wallet
pawn ticket, draft notice
jaywalking summons.

Compressible eyes
from poker chips
to pulpy slits.

# CROSSING 116TH STREET

All day I've laid up in the park
on 108th and Second Ave
creating a masterpiece of a high:
slugging Ballantine Ale,
toking Panama Red,
*tragos* of *Ron Llave*,
two rounds of dugee,
three rounds of coke,
a gobble of goofballs,
cold swigs of Rhythm,
and a head-soaring huff
of Amyl-Nitrate.

It's approaching 5 o'clock.
I need to mellow down,
meet my lady who just got out of work.
She's been on me about my sloppy ways
under the influence:
talking two octaves above or below
my natural range,
scratching my pubes in front of her pops,
passing out on the subway,
losing hats, wallets and wristwatches.

I'm ready to book
when my roommate breezes by,
hands me a sugar cube,
says 15,000 mics of acid.
I say, yeah, right
and pop it in my mouth.

Who's Pat jiving—
he hasn't had anything in ages
that packs a punch—
his weed is sugar and oregano,
his hash, opium incense,
his coke and dope, all milk sugar.

An hour later I'm cool but kicking:
going high dome on my lady
with philosophy and politics,
cracking jokes that have her pleading
with me to stop or she'll pee on herself,
mugging and making voice imitations
of her favorite movie stars.

We're crossing 116th Street.
I'm digging Cantinflas' name
on the marquee of the Cosmos Theater
when a car goes by blasting
"Boogaloo Blues" by Johnny Colón
and I realize I can no longer move,
feet stuck in pink peanut butter,
skin peeling off my arms
exposing bones, tendons, muscles.

I'm shivering.
The sky is black.
It's raining drops of blood.
The wind howls through my veins.
I hear a voice far away:
"Baby, baby, what's wrong?
Watch out for the cars!
Get out of the street!
Come on, are you crazy?"

Pat's acid is on! It's real!
Roaches pour out of my eyes.
Rats run through my intestines.
I'm being dragged like a statue
across the street.
In between horn blasts
I see Mexican sombreros
the size of circus tents,
hat bands filled with sharks' teeth.

# Righteous Fiend

Let me tell you about Papo.
He had "No Hope Without Dope"
tattooed on his left arm
and in the crotch of his right
a tattoo of a naked lady
with her legs wide open
and where her bush
should have been,
a big scabby mound
he lifted up to stick his spike in
every time he got off.

# THE APOSTLES' CREED

Pat hadn't been out of stir too long
for armed robbery when I met him
selling loose joints in a school yard.
All smiles, with a come-on-in-whites
are-welcome-too approach.
I bought two bones
and followed him to a bench
where I drank from his emerald-green
jug of Ballentine Ale
and he rolled me a *bomba,*
a reefer fat as a frankfurter.

The schoolyard was alive
with small drug dealers hawking
loosies, tres and nickle bags.
Pat knew them all,
beseeched them all
in Spanish and English:
*"Hermanos,"* he said, "put aside
your petty differences,
throw your scrawny savings
in a common kitty
so we can buy bulk, save money,
pump up our profits."

The dealers laughed,
looked at Pat like he was loony,
kept their chump change in their pockets.

By the summer's end
Pat and I had gotten tight enough
to become roommates.
He coaxed me into giving him my last
paycheck before starting college
so he could buy a pound of pot.

75

In a month he had doubled his investment,
in two months tripled it,
and by the time spring came he'd become
the schoolyard's main connection.

He called the drug dealers
who copped from him
The Apostles
and laid down the six sacred rules:
No adding catnip or oregano to the weed.
No Apostle can undersell another Apostle.
No chumping the white folks.
Everyone sounds the alarm against the pigs.
Everyone gets down and stomps
the stash-stealers and stick-up artists.
Narco through the nose not the needle.

Things went well at first,
everyone in the school yard
followed Pat's preaching,
pulled their weight,
profits were up and bullshit was down.
Then the sniffers began to skin-pop,
the skin-poppers began to vein-jolt,
perps cut deals with pigs,
customers fleeced, set up, mugged.

And on the home front
I tapped Pat's bundle, looted his kitty.
Pat split our crib,
prowled the school yard
looking for Apostles
who beat him for consignment money,
ending up back in stir
after a bungled bodega robbery.

# FASHIONISTA

He crashes in the coal bin
of a deserted building
paper patch over one eye
blackened rags for clothes
but Fernando Cruz
formerly known as Dandy Nandy
was once such a lady's man
that when he first took the needle
he'd tie up with an Oscar de la Renta
garter belt clenched in his teeth
lace noose between bulging veins.

# SHOOTING DOPE WITH TROTSKY

I score some hefty bags of scag
from Old Man Cano on East 118th Street
the *viejito*—40 plus years in the dope game—
who once ODed on Christmas Eve
and leaned into a radiator
leaving a burn scar down the middle of his head.

I rush to the East Village
and buy a mess of Trotskyite newspapers:
*Vanguard, Fighting Worker, Theory and Practice,*
march into a N.Y.U. bathroom
lock myself up in a vast marble stall
and pump Cano's sacks into my arm.

After reading competing accounts
of the 1921 Kronkstadt rebellion,
the Minneapolis Teamster Strike of 1934,
I nod off to the lullaby
of *The ABC of Materialist Dialectics,*
the negation, of the negation, of the negation.

# CALLING ALL DOPERS

Caught short on the street
without the wherewithal
to filter your get-high?
Afraid of pumping impurities
into your ticker?

Don't panic! Improvise!
Remember the society of mainliners
are among Gotham's
most resourceful citizens.

Go to your nearest public telephone,
unscrew the talking end of the receiver,
pinch off a piece of cotton wadding inside
and roll it like a snot ball between
thumb and forefinger.

Later at your favorite bathroom,
basement, or rooftop
drop the cotton into your cooker,
add the requisite amounts
of white powder and water
and simmer until soupy.

Then jitter free
jab your spike into Ma Bell's
makeshift dirt screen
and strap-up aboard
the jet plane to Nodsville.

# CHOCO PLAYS THE PALADIUM

To Alfredo "Chocolate" Armenteros

When Choco plays a solo
He tilts the trumpet
Towards the south pole
Fingers fluttering the valves
Notes building up
And cascading down
A burst steam pipe
A pool of molasses
Time and tone shuffling
then reshuffling the dancers' feet

# COCOON COZY

I knew the dope was dyno
because when my connect left
I went through his stash
and swiped a packet of pure
shit that could be stepped on
five times or more.

I knew he'd figure out
who robbed him
and with a couple of goons
come gunning for me
but I didn't give a fuck,
fed up with shooting Pepsi—
I really wanted to FEEL SOMETHING.

I knew I had to be cool,
couldn't get greedy,
so I just took a pinch
the size of a match head
and in my furnished room
with my coat still on
threw half in my wine cap cooker.

I knew I was in trouble
soon as I hit myself off,
the pins and needles
prickling my forearms,
the darkness filling my head,
my body sinking like a crate of bricks.

I knew I couldn't wait,
not even a second,
and turning on the shower,
threw myself in,
clothes and all,
and after forty-five minutes
of freezing water
kept myself from ODing.

I knew the sun always
follows the rain and chain-smoked
on the edge of my bed,
my head bobbing down
to my shoelaces cradled in a snuggly glow.

I knew it was late
and I was hungry when I rolled up
my lids. Seven hours had gone by.
Outside only a Carvel was open
and I chowed down on a vanilla shake
and fudge-dripping banana boat.

Back in my crib
I knew it couldn't get better
but feeling a bit blasé,
a decimal down from cocoon cozy,
I put another pinch in the cooker
and with an eye on my shower
pumped the P in my arm.

# JUNKIE'S ALARM CLOCK

Incoming tide
of fever flashes
floods last night's
silky womb.

Pitching pot
belly acid and unlatch
-able asshole
propel feet
towards curds of
putrescence
caking shithouse floor.

# DOPEFIENDERY

We both go
to the rooftop.
I put the dope
in the cooker.
He puts water
in the cooker.
I put a match
under the cooker.
He pulls out
his spike.
I put my spike
in the cooker.
He sits
on a milk crate.
I shoot the dope
into a vein.
He sits and watches.
I fall to the floor,
spike in my arm.
He sits
and watches.
I thrash around
on broken glass.
He sits and
watches.
I bleed from
a hundred cuts.
He sits
and watches.
I stiffen,
turn blue.
He puts his spike

in the cooker.
I turn a deep shade
of purple.
He shoots the dope
in his arm.
I gasp
for breath.
He rifles
my pants' pockets.
I begin convulsing.
He says,
good,
greedy cocksucker
and leaves.

# A Doper's Prayer

Oh Lord, thank you
for my morning fix.

May my game be strong,
the suckers plentiful,
the dope top shelf.

Protect me from AIDS,
abscesses, honest cops,
Hep C, drug counselors,
ODs, missionary priests,
and cutthroat junkies.

Keep my cooker clean,
my spike sharp,
my veins from collapsing.

Oh Lord, may the peace
of the long nod be with me.

# TIES

Pedro is unemployed,
hates his step-father,
steals his black and white TV,
cops *una bolsita de cinco pesos,*
ties up with his trouser belt
and *curarse.*

Ruby works in a sweat shop,
hates her supervisor,
sells dresses on the side,
cops a ten dollar pack,
ties up with a nylon stocking
and gets off.

Aldo manages a tailor shop,
hates his immigrant patrons,
pads their bills,
cops ten two-dollar caps,
ties up with a silk necktie
and takes off.

Miss Kim is a case worker,
hates welfare recipients,
denies them benefits,
cops a quarter of an ounce,
ties up with a piece of clothesline
and hits herself off.

Sean is a bartender,
hates his white-collar customers,
waters down their drinks,
cops a bundle of dope,
ties up with electrical cord
and cranks up.

Sarah Jane is a nurse,
despises drug addicts,
herself included,
steals morphine vials,
ties up with rubber tubing
and fixes.

# STICKY BUNS

After a heavy day
of hustling:
      robbing newspapers
before dawn,
hawking them to sidewalk vendors
for two bucks a bundle,
      swiping an electric shaver
at Woolworth's and downing it
for 4 dollars
at Bebo's Barber Shop,
      running Downtown
and panhandling $3.17
in front of the Astor Place subway station,
      collecting *chavito*—spare change
from Tito, Nandy,
Negro, Frenchie,
Naomi, Milagros,
      pinching packs of *cigarillos*
from candy stores
and selling loosies
for five cents a piece,
      cashing in soda bottles,
      carrying old people's groceries,
      selling fake jewelry,
      shilling and
      steering customers to dealers,
      renting out my gimmicks
for a dollar a pop,

after four bum bags,
three decent tastes,
and a late afternoon jolt
of "dealer's cut"
from Papote's private stock,
I'm ready to chow down.

I go to Tata's Spanish Bakery
on Lex and 104th,
buy a sticky bun for a nickel.
It's three times the size
of my fist and fits into my belly
like an expandable sea sponge.
I wash it down with a 16-ounce jug
of Big Blue 100 percent synthetic
blueberry soda.

A block away I barf
for the first time,
a sudsy ejaculation
that lets me know
the dope is still kicking.
After vomiting the third time
I'm ready for the evening's
festivities in the park,
my stomach filled enough
with the sticky bun
to hold me until tomorrow.

# Blood Oath

I never resigned myself to being a junkie
never put myself on the same level as the fiends
in East Harlem where I live, that scurvy bunch
selling their babies' jewelry for a fix,
walking around in tee-shirts
with fly-clustered scabs in the pits of their arms.

I grew up in middle class Connecticut
attended military college.
In my family nobody was poor.
In my family nobody stole.
In my family nobody wanted for anything.

I never resigned myself
to being a junkie.
I've chucked my works
out the window a thousand times
swearing to God
I'll never get high again.

Once I even cut my finger
and on a piece of paper
wrote in my own blood:
"I swear to my mother,
my grandmother,
my unborn children
that starting tomorrow
I won't get high any more."
But by Thursday morning I was back
rummaging in the alleyway for my works again.

# THE RESURRECTIONIST

Needles
in necks,
arms, groins.

Frenchie catches
an OD,
hits the ground.

The undead
step
over him.

Petey,
ex-gang leader
Golden Gloves champ

unties
a yellow bandana
from around his neck

wipes his face,
crouches down,
crosses

Frenchie's arms
on his chest,
straightens

his legs,
pulls
on his feet.

Frenchie's
chest quivers,
eyes open,

blue lips
bend
into a smile.

# Caucasian Cool

My ex-roommate Pat had a way
of rolling the vowels of my last name
while lowering his voice
suggesting my connection
to the Gambino, Genovese,
or other blood and guts Mafia families.

A drug peddler by profession,
he'd invite customers to our crib,
put out a spread of bodega-bought
salami and cheese, Italian bread,
olives with pimientos,
pour Gallo port into plastic glasses.

I'd sit around in a guinea-tee,
Madonna medallion round my neck,
black hair slicked-back,
the bristles—of what Pat called—
my pussy-tickler moustache,
menacing as cactus needles.
I'd barely mouth a word
until we finished the grit
and sampled Pat's products.
Then I was all praise:
the weed tripped me out,
the coke made my eyeballs clatter,
the dope dropped my head
like a dead tulip.

Everything was copacetic
until my heroin habit took over
and I clipped Pat's stash once too often.
When he cut out on me

I lost my protector,
my cover,
the single most powerful force
that enabled me to finesse
the cutthroat dope scene of El Barrio.

With Pat by my side
I'd been Caucasian cool,
an OK guy,
one of the fellows,
to be untouched by predators
unless they wanted to face
a fist-blow or bullet.

But when he bailed out
my Mafia veneer vaporized
and I joined the rest of the junkies
in their money-grubbing games:
borrowing with no intention of paying,
panhandling,
renting my gimmicks for a taste,
downing counterfeit bills,
selling swag, bum bags,
stealing, swindling.

Then the locals peeped my hole card:
a *blanquito* dopefiend
outsider, with no guardian,
no back up,
and without the *cojones*
to carry a gun.
Then after being bullied,
beat for money, dope, and stolen goods,
sneered and spat at,
I fled El Barrio and begged my way back
to my folks' house
in Vanillaville, Connecticut.

# PRIMO'S BOTÁNICA

Doping down in El Barrio,
Tito and I chump the dealers:
stiffing them for consignment,
slipping them funny money,
stealing their stashes,
until they send their *cañoneros*
with shiny shivs
to shank us
and throw our bodies
on mounds of rotting chicken parts
behind the butcher shops of the Marketa.

We lay low:
I move back with my folks
to suburban Connecticut.
Tito holes up in his grandmother's crib
in the shadows of the Park Avenue El.
To put together our cop money
I forage nearby swamps for:
bullfrogs
spring peepers
pickerel frogs
toads
delivering them on weekends to Tito
who sells them for a buck a pop
at *Primo's Botánica*
where they will be ground into
good luck potions.

1969

# MUZZLED

Right in front of the cute cashier
in the hill-top restaurant,
chin-bearded Toni the Butch
sticks her hands down my pants
to see if her puppy is alive and kicking.
I keep my mouth shut
since she carries a Cuban pig-sticker
and just lent me ten dollars in rolled-up pennies
to keep the hungry dogs of dope at bay.

# THE INTERVIEW

It's a night-dark November morning.
I'm at the bottom of a stairway
somewhere in the South Bronx
at a drug program called Logos.
My face has an orange sheen
like axle grease. I shiver
from the icy drafts blowing through
my golf jacket, the only
outer garment I own.

My bony ass is sore
from sitting on a wooden bench.
I want to split but remember:
ripping off students' books
while they sat in the cafeteria,
selling my father's stamp collection,
OD'ing on a rooftop,
carried down by dopefiends,
arms pinned behind my back,
hands tearing at my wallet,
my shirt, my shoes.

I think about waking up
with red ants in my marrow,
racing to the toilet,
vomit running through my nose,
the wad of shit in my throat.

Two hours go by,
I'm faint, vision blurred.
I want to leave but Nilsa warned me
—no more chances—
if I don't get into Logos
she's gone for good.
I hear whispers, laughter,
the echo of a piano and vibraphone,

a voice singing
"*...ratón, el ratón!*"

People go up and down the stairs
staring at me. I ask somebody
for a smoke and they look away.

Finally, a man comes—
sheared hair, missing teeth.
"Follow me," he says.
"What took so long?" I ask.
"We're a family here; we want to see
how bad you want to get in."

At the interview I tell
a woman with a scar across her face,
how I'd done social work in East Harlem.
I tell a black man with an eye patch,
how I lost my moorings.
I tell an Italian guy with a withered hand,
I can't take it anymore.

The woman shouts: liar, loser.
The black guy calls me a racist.
The Italian says I'm a white Uncle Tom.
My interviewers stand up,
leave the room.

I have no money,
no place to go.
I debate running
out the door, throwing myself
under a bus.

I hear branches bang
against the windows.
It's beginning to rain.
In two days
it will be Thanksgiving.

# Hands-On

The doctor says cancer, and Nellie runs to Doña Alba
who says forget the M.D., it's *brujeria*—witchcraft—
and a *limpieza*—spiritual cleaning—is what you need.

Doña Alba rubs Nellie's body with dragon's
blood oil, drenches her with *Agua de Florida,*
and sets Nellie's nightgown on fire while making
the sign of the cross with a votive candle.

After the screams, the police batter down the door,
find Nellie a blackened heap, Alba by her side,
mumbling prayers, fingers like blistered franks.

# THE MEAT RACK

She stood out with her dyed-black, pixie hairdo,
candle-white skin, so gaunt
her eyes looked like golf balls.
Whenever I got off the subway
at 125th and Lex—my home stop—
she'd be there
a regular among the prostitutes.

I had the typical male junkie
reaction to female addicts:
they disgusted me.
As I'd exit the station
I'd keep my head down,
making a dash past the meat rack.

In spite of my disguise
—Kangol cap, oval shades, moustache, and chin beard—
the hookers had that extra sense,
knew I was an outsider, *un blanquito,*
would come on to me like I was a trick:
"*¡Mira, chico, la salsa caliente!*"
"Yo, baby, let mamma cool ya!"

Five blocks away in my railroad flat
I still wasn't free of them.
One lived in the apartment above
and I'd hear her pimp smacking her
at all hours of the day and night.

"Get up off my money, bitch,
or I'll put my shoe up your ass."
The ceiling would shake, sending down

flakes of plaster causing my neighbors
to joke that it snowed in my crib
even in the summer time.

After I entered Logos
I was joined several weeks later
by the pixie-cut from 125th Street.
I watched her do a makeover
new hairdo, new teeth,
a young boyfriend.
But at the end of the program
she got pregnant and deciding
she couldn't handle a kid
went to Lincoln Hospital—known
as the Butcher Shop by locals—
to have an abortion
and after being given an anesthesia
contraindicated by her asthma,
died on the operating table.

At Ortiz's Funeral Home
on East 103rd Street
by the black wall of the Park Avenue El
I waited until everyone in our program
paid their respects, then joined
the whores in saying goodbye.

Back in the South Bronx,
shades drawn tight,
shadows like boa constrictors,
someone said, "Shit, we're all on borrowed time."
Still I saw traces of light
left by the pixie cut meat-racker.

# ON THE ROOF

of the Bronx rehab,
under a sky stretching
from Springdale to Spanish Harlem,

BB-riddled frogs, broken school
windows, Christmas day raids
on my aunts' pocketbooks.

The sun warms my face.
No throbbing bones, cramps
in my gut, cesspool saliva.

I've no cravings now,
thankful for a full belly,
and a safe night's sleep.

Around the corner
hooded drug dealers
stand in charred doorways.

Tires thump on cobblestones
wind down to an intersection
with a dead traffic light and no traffic.

# CHINO

Chino met Pat at Sing Sing
and visits our crib everyday
now that Pat slings *material:*
*perico,* ups, downs, hash, dope.
Chino goes for the super-resinated
Bolivian Thunder-Buds
and while usually broke
comes by with a quart or two
of Rheingold or Millers High Life.

When Pat brings over some Queens gals
Chino chooses the plump Sicilian
named Santa Maria
who has a good bank job
while I go for the Jamaican
with the ebony-wasp body
claiming to be an art student.

Chino shakes his head
when I offer him a hit
of dope from a sandwich bag
of Paul's uncut stash.
"I'm telling you," he says,
between pot puffs,
"You better watch yourself;
that shit's going to sneak up on you."

I laugh.
I've heard Chino's story:
He was a junkie, cat burglar,
did two five-year bids Upstate
for grand larceny, and while

incarcerated joined the Black Muslims
who cured him of his dope habit,
then broke with the Muslims
when he was set free
because they rejected his girlfriend,
a blue-eyed devil.

Two years later I'm in a Bronx rehab
a few blocks from the Italian neighborhood
of Arthur Avenue three months sober
with nothing but a head-full
of treatment slogans,
and a Salvation Army-bought
blue blazer on my back,
when I run into Chino
carrying a bag of groceries.

We slap five.
Chino asks me if I want
to fire up a dynamite stick of weed.
"Nah," I tell him, "I can't handle it."
He gives me his home address.
"Come over and visit anytime."
A week later I'm on Arthur Avenue
hustling food donations for the program
and decide to drop by Chino's.
Inside I hear a kid cry.
I knock softly.
Santa Maria opens the door
sees my face
closes the door
turns the lock twice.

# LA BOTÁNICA

In memory of Arsenio Rodriguez

Leaving Puerto Rico penniless, children in hand,
Marisol came to New York, four years after her husband,
convinced he had a *corteja*—another woman.

To keep from poisoning him, or jumping in front of a subway,
she went to the Santa Bárbara Botánica
for potions, charms, and *consultas.*

It was there Marisol first saw the blind black man
with the gold chain draped across his tie, *"No me llores más*
—Don't Cry Anymore," moaning out of an old phonograph.

She knew he was Cuban because when a bug buzzed by
he said, *"Mira, un bicho,"* causing Marisol to blush;
where she came from *bicho* meant the male sex organ.

Sometimes the blind man sat on a wooden chair on the sidewalk
surrounded by his fans who called him Don Arsenio,
and begged him to make music.

He played the *tres*—the Cuban guitar—with *gran sentimiento*
and people accompanied him, using sticks and coins,
turning fruit crates and soda bottles into percussion instruments.

Often the music moved Marisol and she swayed her hips.
And when the blind man heard her dress rustling
he would wink in her direction.

Once when Marisol entered the store in tears,
her hair wild as weeds, he gave her an empty rum bottle
stuffed with branches of herbs.

"Put your husband's hair inside," he said,
"along with your own urine and shake the bottle
when you suspect he is with another woman."

After the blind man left, Marisol learned he was
"*El Ciego Maravilloso*"—The Marvelous Blind Man—
creator of the Cuban *conjunto* and father of the mambo.

Marisol kept his bottle on an altar between two burning candles.
"*Mi apesta la vida*—my life stinks," she said and as time went on,
she cared less and less about her husband's running around.

She said his betrayals were only one thorn in a cursed life.
She missed her sisters in Puerto Rico, hated her Harlem railroad flat,
raised sons who moved out of state and daughters who did the same.

"*Tengo el Diablo dentro*—I have the devil inside," she raved.
And when her husband tried to drag her to a doctor,
she smashed *El Ciego Maravilloso's* bottle over his head.

At her funeral, two of her husband's sons from his *corteja*
showed up, one of them a conga player dressed all in white,
the room filling with the smell of gardenias and coconuts.

# PILE OF PINS

His name was Moisés—Moses in English—
and with his scruffy beard, sun-burned skin,
and passionate patter,
he could pass as a Hebrew prophet.

He swung into Logos on crutches
and hadn't been there a hot minute
before he told us about the pins
the doctors had put in his toes.
He was kicking cold turkey
and in between retching and the runs
he let us look at his feet
with their wiry protuberances
resembling porcupine spines.

He gave us the scoop:
he'd been on his knees under a stairwell
on Saint Ann's Avenue
shooting up some Mexican brown
when he OD'ed and fell over backwards
cutting off the circulation
in his lower legs and feet
causing his toes to wither
from near-gangrene.

Logos had only been open
a couple of months
and while the residents patched the roof,
plastered the ceilings,
repaired the stairways,
doing what they could
to get the ramshackle tenement

into livable shape, Moses rested on his crutches
and boasted of his plumbing skills,
carpentry skills, electrical skills,
swore that as soon as he got his Medicaid card
and had his operation
he'd show us how to rehab our slum building
from basement to attic.

Two days after his surgery
while we were asleep
Moses packed up his bags and disappeared.
He took with him the one-speaker stereo,
the power drill, tool box, wrench set,
cleared out from our freezer
the Thanksgiving turkeys
donated by the local A&P,
removed the clock
from the group room wall.

The staff struck back,
turned our material loss
into a therapeutic gain.
The silver pins found at the bottom
of Moses' bed
were fit into the crown
of a frilly gold bonnet
residents were made to wear
as a learning experience
if caught taking
an unauthorized cracker, cookie,
or cup of coffee.

# FLUTEFLIRTING

To Don Gonzalo Fernández

He points his flute at her.
She smiles from the dance floor.

He brings the embouchure to his mouth.
She peels away from her partner.

He slurs three chords in low C.
She glides forward.

He soars upward, fingers blur the keys.
She loosens her arms, sways her hips.

He trills at the end of an arpeggio.
Her shoulders shake, nipples harden.

He flutter-tongues high G.
Her legs tremble, eyes close.

He ends after a drum roll.
Her partner walks up to her.

He lowers his flute, drains his saliva.
She jumps at the touch of her partner's hand.

# CORE

To Israel "Cachao" López

Peeling an apple listening to
*"Cachao y su ritmo caliente"*
bass beat powering my blade into pulp,
guiro's rasp paring skin away,
Tata Güines' conga hacking at the *corazón,*
stems drop, seeds fly,
Alejandro's trumpet flourish,
and four pieces of apple glisten on a plate.

# DEATH OF A SOBERTONE

Two weeks after he left Logos
I took the call.
"He's dead!" his mother hollered,
"James is dead!"
Crash. She hung up the phone.

He'd been found by some
cardboard boxes near a prostitute's stroll
alongside Bruckner Boulevard.
The police report read death
by heroin overdose.

Our first meeting: his shirt
with the ripped pocket,
his wide hips and rough laughter
that made his belly roll,
the burn scar cutting a swath
alongside his high Afro.

After six months of therapy,
he still wouldn't say how he'd gotten burned
though a rumor claimed he'd been blow-torched
after robbing a drug dealer.

I came up with the idea of forming a trio
after hearing James sing
"Sitting on the Dock of the Bay."
I took tenor, Roger baritone, and James
with the most soulful voice took lead.
Our fellow residents dubbed us the Sobertones.

We sang "Try a Little Tenderness,"
"Pain in My Heart,"
"Mr. Pitiful,"
at house parties, barbeques,
morning meetings, the residents cheered us on,
found any excuse to hear us harmonize.

But the director snubbed us,
claimed we should raise our octave
above street-corner crooning and pabulum poetry,
soar with jazz and the classics.

Then the director did a room run,
found a pair of James' pants
with bologna slices in the pockets.
He demanded an example be made
of James' dopefiend gluttony,
had his head shaved,
ordered him to sleep in the bathtub
wearing pink gloves and a pig's mask.

When James complained about sleeplessness
Roger and I were ordered to hold open the front door
while the director threw him out,
tossing his suitcase across Washington Avenue.

I swallowed hard, remembered Otis Redding's
plane going down in a lake in Wisconsin,
worried how the show would go on.

# THE DEPUSIFICATION CHAMBER

The counselors call us:
junkies,
hypes, hopheads,
low-lifes, death-trippers
zombies,
day-one-dingbats
to undo our denial,
batter down our defenses,
raze our resistance
to a new level-headed,
positive lifestyle.

They say our bellies
brim with poison
from all the abuse
we've heaped on ourselves
and send us to therapy groups
where we barf our bad feelings,
let fly our toxins
by calling each other:
junkies,
hypes, hopheads,
lowlifes, death-trippers,
zombies,
day-one-dingbats.

When we back-slide
and return
to our dopefiend ways:
stay out beyond curfew,
talk more than ten minutes on the phone,
take an extra slice of bacon
at breakfast,
the counselors give us creative
learning experiences,
put guys in dresses,

gals in garbage barrels,
shave our heads,
make us hold cigarette lighters
while wearing diapers
with signs around our necks saying
"Help me!
I'm a flaming asshole."

After six months in the program
I become a junior counselor
and get the chance
to give as good as I've gotten.
When a paesan' named Fabio
enters the program
and won't stop mumbling under
his breath when being told
what to do
I call him:
junkie,
hype, hophead,
low-life, death-tripper,
zombie,
day-one-dingbat.

When Fabio doesn't stop
I make him stand
in a utility closet
to lance his psychic boils,
dub it the "Depusification Chamber"
have him recite at morning meetings
little ditties like
"No hugs for me,
I'm pus-primed
and ready to blow."
Three months after he leaves Logos
Fabio calls me
still mumbling under his breath
from a psyche ward
at Bellevue.

# THE QUEEN OF LATIN SOUL

To Guadalupe "La Lupe" Yoli

Tito Puente breaks into a solo,
his drum sticks like sea foam
slathering the shore line.

La Lupe lifts her dress up,
bends at the edge of the stage,
breasts out, swirling a lavender scarf.

The crowd at Madison Square Garden
jumps to its feet, cheering.
Paul pumps his hips.

"She's sniffing coke
under her fingernails," he yells
through his hands.

Carlota glares at her Irish husband.
They met in a drug program
and married when she became pregnant.

"Let's see some beaver, Chiquita,"
he yells, getting into a shoving match
with two Puerto Ricans.

Carlota grabs his arm.
"You're drunk, let's go."
"Fuck off!"

"Figures you'd side with your people,"
he says, fingers in his mouth, whistling,
La Lupe blowing kisses at her fans.

# THE WHITE LADY

Pito straightens his back and pops his eyes open
as the young woman with a butterscotch pony tail
and baggy fatigue pants unlocks the gate and enters
the community garden on the corner of East 104th street.

*¡Esa puta sucia!* he says to himself.
*After all those years of calling the neighborhood a slum*
*the blanquitos now want to cross 96th Street and take what's ours.*

Pito's head wavers, his eyes close, and he sinks
toward the sidewalk where his battered radio
with the twisted coat hangar for an antenna
blasts the theme song to Nando's Latin Nostalgia Show.

Pito shakes his shoulders, his feet glued to the ground,
the chorus of "Let's Get Stoned" by the Lebrón Brothers
awakens his memories of the 60's, the boss times before ODs,
shoot-outs, AIDS, and heavy duty time Upstate
had taken so many of his crimies.

His mind wanders back to crowded shooting galleries
on rooftops and basements just down the block,
to dyno deuce bags of *estufa* that kept him *teniendo una nota cabrona*—
good and fucked up—
to liquid amphetamine sealed in glass tubes called *bombitas.*

He remembers the easy pinches in clothing stores
before electronic security devices made pickings slim,
his all day heroin hard-on that kept the square girls screaming
and their pocketbooks open, the dopefiend sweethearts
that would always turn a trick for him if he was uptight for a fix.

The sounds from his radio go fuzzy and Pito
lowers himself butt first like he's taking a slow motion dump
and adjusts the antenna. The static clears
and the heavy 'bone sound of Johnny Colón's
"You Gotta Love Me" accompanies his ascent.

He thinks back to some paddy girls,
social worker types that lived on the block in the 60's,
how they tried to get him to stop scagging,
how one of them—Fran—even had tears in her eyes
when she saw him nodding an hour after he'd come out of detox.

It made him feel good someone cared about him
but what a lame Fran was, she didn't realize
that he never went to detox to stay away from stuff
but only to clean up enough so that the next time he got off
he could really feel something.

The old songs: *"Qué Te Pedí"* by La Lupe,
"Ran-Can-Can" by Tito Puente, *"Justicia"* by Eddie Palmieri
pour out of his radio. *¡Coño!* he rasps, shaking his shoulders.
He'd seen all the great acts at one time or another
and mamboed with the best of them
until the White Lady became his only partner
and the junkie jig his only dance.

A metal door clangs shut and Pito opens his eyes again,
sees the blonde locking the garden gate,
her ponytail bouncing as she heads towards
the 103rd Street subway station.

*Esa maricona*, he says to himself, eyes closing,
*who is she to lock me out;*
*'spose I want to cop a squat,*
*check out the daisies*
*while I nip a little Night Train.*

# Beyond

# PAT DANCES TO THE SOUL MAKOSSA

Joint glowing between his teeth,
his Afro with the ax cleft part sways
to the Swahili chant and shuffling beat.

Shoulders rolling, coke spoon bouncing
on bronze fishnet tee shirt,
his hips swivel slowly.

Trumpets sound off, sax gallops,
he drops his hands to his knees,
head camel-walking through smoke rings.

# Spa Ha

Stalactites of Murano glass
under the Park Avenue El.

Car horns meow, bark and chirp.

Women in surgical gowns
sell bean curd *cuchifritos.*

Cops and parole officers sit on
hydrants fitted with Tex Tan saddles.

Mechanical dragonflies toot
*"Cielito Lindo"* on platinum flutes.

A 40-story hotel mimics
a quart bottle of Havana Club.

The Museum of Smells features
rumba pumps, rancid lard, cilantro,
burned plaster board, rooming house toilets.

# SURVIVORS

Friends since that day forty years ago.

My long climb up the narrow staircase
dope sick, suicidal.

You welcoming me with a firm
hand and welfare-issue brogans.

Now flaky gray house
shut tighter than a mummy's fist.

Silence where there had been manicky
motion, bug-outs and hug-outs.

Silence of those who didn't make it.

# A Rooster Crows in El Barrio

and a uniformed doorman falls
through an open manhole

a repossessed car explodes
when the bank agent turns the ignition key

a sidewalk preacher is electrocuted
plugging in a loud speaker

the manager of Wendy's slips
face first into a tub of cooking oil

plainclothes detectives shoot
each other during a bomb scare

a landlord is asphyxiated
by roach spray in a windowless bathroom

a philanthropist strangles
on a bone at a fund raising dinner

# LITANY OF SAN VITO

*To Congressman Vito Marcantonio (1901-1954)*

San Vito of East Harlem                    Pray for us
San Vito bread of the poor                 Pray for us
San Vito crucified by Wall Street          Pray for us
San Vito martyr of McCarthyism             Pray for us

From the jail cell walls                   San Vito deliver us
From the backyard crap game                San Vito deliver us
From the loan shark's vig                  San Vito deliver us
From the drunken stupor                    San Vito deliver us
From TB and asthma                         San Vito protect us
From the social worker's visit             San Vito protect us
From immigration raids                     San Vito protect us
From the landlord's greed                  San Vito protect us

# Water Games

Humacao, Puerto Rico, 1971

Sunset, a blaze of purple and pink.
Nilsa takes two slugs of Bacardi,
throws the bottle into the incoming tide.
The race is on, I swim out,
grab the jug before Jack, unscrew the cap,
take a gulp, toss the bottle back into the sea.
Battling breakers, jellyfish,
lengthening shadows of night,
the three of us chase the green glass,
swimming and swilling, until, in total darkness,
Jack flounders in the foam of the shoreline,
Nilsa passes out in the backseat of the car,
and I flooring the gas pedal, sink tires into the sand.

# GLOSSARY

## A

| | |
|---|---|
| ¡Adelante! | Forward! Go Ahead! |
| ¡Así camina! | That's how to do it! |
| ¡Así se baile! | That's how to dance! |

## B

| | |
|---|---|
| bailador | dancer |
| blanquito | whitey, white person |
| bomba | thick marijuana cigarette |
| bone | marijuana cigarette |
| borracho | drunk |

## C

| | |
|---|---|
| caballo | horse, heroin |
| cabrón | cuckold |
| calabaza | calabash, pumpkin |
| chévere | cool, great |
| cintura | waist |
| cojones | testicles, balls |
| ¡Coño! | damn |
| corazón | heart, core |
| crimie | crime partner, close friend |
| curarse | to take a fix |

## D

| | |
|---|---|
| dugee | heroin |
| deuce | two dollar bag of heroin |

## E

| | |
|---|---|
| enchulada | madly in love |
| esa puta sucia | that dirty whore |
| esa maricona | that faggot |
| estufa | heroin |

## G

| | |
|---|---|
| ganja | marijuana |
| guanguancó | Cuban rhythm |

## H

| | |
|---|---|
| H | heroin |
| ¡Hasta la victoria! | Until victory! |
| head | drug user |
| hermanos | brothers |
| hombro | shoulder |
| hole card | card dealt face down in stud poker, something hidden, |
| hophead, hype, hypo | dopefiend |

## I

| | |
|---|---|
| italianos perros | Italian dogs |

## K

| | |
|---|---|
| kick sticks | marijuana cigarettes |

## L

| | |
|---|---|
| loosies | loose joint |

## M

| | |
|---|---|
| machatero | machete-wielder |
| manteca | lard, heroin |

## N

| | |
|---|---|
| nada | nothing |
| niños | children |

## P

| | |
|---|---|
| P | pure |
| paddy | whitey, white person |
| perico | parakeet, cocaine |
| pimp's dust | cocaine |
| piragüero | snow cone seller |
| por siempre | forever |
| pura basura | pure garbage |
| pureza | purity |

## Q

| | |
|---|---|
| *¡Qué rico!* | So good! |

## S

| | |
|---|---|
| *¡Sacude!* | Shake! |
| *salsa na' ma'* | nothing but Latin music |
| *salsero* | lover/dancer of Latin music |
| scagging | getting high on heroin |
| skin popping | injecting into the skin |
| squat | seat |

## T

| | |
|---|---|
| *tecato* | heroin, heroin addict |
| *todas las muchachos/as* | all the boys /girls |
| *tragos* | swallows |
| tragic magic | heroin |
| tres | three dollar bags of heroin |

## V

| | |
|---|---|
| *¡Vámanos! ¡Vaya!* | Let's go! |

## Y

| | |
|---|---|
| *yerba* | marijuana |

# Discography

*"La Reina Isabel,"* Orquesta Aragón.
*"La Cucaracha,"* Traditional Mexican Folk Song.
*"Azúcar,"* Eddie Palmieri y La Perfecta.
*"Jala Jala Boogaloo,"* Ricardo Ray.
*"Contigo,"* Los Panchos."
*"Sí Sí No No,"* Machito and His Afro-Cuban Orchestra.
"I Like It Like That," Pete Rodrigues.
"Acid," Ray Barretto.
*"Trompeta en Montuno,"* Alfredo "Chocolate" Armenteros.
"Deserie," The Charts.
"Wind," The Jesters.
"Gloria," The Cadillacs.
*"Oye Como Va,"* Tito Puente.
"Swinging With Symphony Sid," King Pleasure.
*"Fortuna,"* King Nando.
"Soul Burst," Cal Tjader.
*"Picadillo,"* Cal Tjader.
"Afro Blue," Cal Tjader.
"Maramoor Mambo," Cal Tjader.
*"Manteca,"* Dizzy Gillepsie.
*"La Esencia de Guaguancó,"* Johnny Pacheco.
"Soul Makossa," Manu Dibango.
"Boogaloo Blues," Johnny Colón.
*"Mama Güela,"* Tito Rodrigues.
*"La Rata,"* Joe Cuba.
*"No Me Llores Más,"* Arsenio Rodrigues y Su Conjunto.
*"El Agua de Clavelitos,"* Gonzalo Fernández.
*"Jóvenes del Ritmo,"* Israel "Cachao" López.
"Sitting On The Dock of the Bay," Otis Redding.
"Try a Little Tenderness," Otis Redding.
"Pain in My Heart," Otis Redding.
"Mr. Pitiful," Otis Redding.
"Let's Get Stoned," Lebrón Brothers.
"You Gotta Love Me," Johnny Colón.
*"Qué Te Pedí,"* La Lupe.
*"Ran-Can-Can,"* Tito Puente.
*"Justicia,"* Eddie Palmieri.

# End Notes

Federico García Lorca (1898-1936)
Possibly the most important Spanish poet and dramatist of the 20th Century, Lorca visited New York for nine months in 1929-30. Inspired by his exploration of Harlem, he wrote several poems about African Americans which were posthumously published in *Poet in New York.*

Julia de Burgos (1914-1953)
Considered by many the greatest poet to have been born in Puerto Rico, de Burgos suffered from alcoholism, depression, and liver disease. She was discovered unconscious on the street in El Barrio and died in Harlem Hospital at the age of 39.

"First Day In El Barrio."
From 1965 until 1967, Cornell University arranged for college students to live in East Harlem for the summer and work as volunteers in tandem with The East Harlem Tenants Council. A student at Pennsylvania Military College at the time, the author participated in the Cornell East Harlem Project in 1966, when his cousin Don Cavellini was student director.

"Fun City."
A nickname for New York City, born when Mayor John Lindsay said during a transit strike in 1966 that he still considered New York a fun city.

"Under the Ferris Wheel"
In 1930 the Italian neighborhood of East Harlem was the largest Italian neighborhood in the United States. At one time up to 500,000 people attended the feast of Our Lady of Mount Carmel Roman Catholic Church on East 115th Street, whose Procession Day is July 16. The author had two uncles who lived there.

"Jefferson Pool"
Built in 1936 and located in Jefferson Park (1st Avenue to FDR, 111th to 114th Streets), it was reconstructed in 1994, and is still in operation today.

"*Manteca*"
Literally, *manteca* means lard in Spanish, but "*Manteca*" is also a song composed by the legendary Cuban conga player Chano Pozo which was made poplular by the Dizzy Gillepsie Orchestra. For a while *manteca* served as a slang word for Afro-Cuban music, a precursor for "salsa." In addition, *manteca* is a popular slang term for both heroin and a female heroin addict.

"The Bathroom at the Village Gate"
The Village Gate (1958-1993) was a nightclub at the corner of Thompson and Bleecker Street in Greenwich Village. Its "Salsa Meets Jazz" series was a seminal part of the history of New York Latin music.

"Crossing 116th Street"
Cantinflas (Mario Moreno Reyes, 1911-1993) was a Mexican-born comedian who was wildly popular throughout Latin America.

"Choco Plays the Palladium."
The Palladium Ballroom (1946-1966), on 53rd Street and 7th Avenue, is New York City's most important Latin music landmark.

"*Primo's Botánica.*"
A *botánica* is a store that deals in herbs and charms used especially by adherents of Santería.

"The Interview."
Logos (1969-1972) was a Bronx-based residential treatment program for drug addicts.

"The Meat Rack."
In the summer of 1970, Carmen Rodrigues, a resident of Logos, died at Lincoln Hospital due to gross malpractice during an abortion. Her death precipitated the takeover of the hospital by a coalition of militant community groups demanding improved medical service.

"Spa Ha"
A new promotional term used by real estate interests to sell and rent properties in Spanish Harlem.

"Litany for Don Vito."
Vito Marcantonio (1901-1953), was the most electorally successful left wing radical in the history of the United States. He lived all his life in East Harlem, and was beloved by his Puerto Rican, Italian, and black constituents. For more information see: *Vito Marcantonio: Radical Politician, 1902-1954*, Gerald Meyer, State University of New York Press, 1989.

# BIOGRAPHY

Gil Fagiani's poetry collection *Rooks* (Rain Mountain Press, 2007) is set at Pennsylvania Military College in the 1960s, his poetry chapbook *Grandpa's Wine* (Poets Wear Prada in 2008) focuses on his family's immigrant genera- tion, and has been translated into Italian by Paul D'Agostino (Poets Wear Prada, pending 2010). His book of poetry *Chianti in Connecticut* was inspired by his childhood in Springdale, Connecticut (Bordighera, pending 2010).

Gil's poems and translations have been published in more than a dozen anthologies, as well as such newspapers and journals as The *New York Times, The Paterson Literary Review, Mudfish, Skidrow Penthouse, Descant, Philadelphia Poets, Identity Theory, Saint Elizabeth Street, The Ledge, Italian Americana, The Journal of Italian Translation,* and *Gradiva.*

He has translated into English, poetry written in Italian, Abruzzese dialect, and Spanish. He co-hosts the monthly open reading of the Italian American Writers' Association at the Cornelia Street Café, and is the Associate Editor of *Feile-Festa: A Literary Arts Journal.*

A social worker (L.C.S.W.) and substance abuse specialist (C.A.S.A.C.) by profession, Gil has directed a residential program for recovering drug addicts and alcoholics in Downtown Brooklyn for the past twenty years.